Fast Food

Written by Sandra Iversen

Illustrated by Bob Kerr

"Come on,"
said Uncle Joe.
"We are going to get
something to eat.
Come on Jake.
Come on Sam.
Come on Pete and Maria."

Jake is eating a hamburger.
Sam is eating a hot dog.
Pete is eating a fishburger.

Uncle Joe said,
"Here is a hamburger, Maria."
"No," said Maria.

Uncle Joe said,
"Here is a fishburger, Maria."
"No," said Maria.

Uncle Joe said,
"Here is a hot dog, Maria."
"No," said Maria.
"Ice cream!
I want ice cream!"

Jake is eating a hamburger. Sam is eating a hot dog. Pete is eating a fishburger.

Maria is not eating.

Uncle Joe is eating
a hamburger,
a fishburger,
and a hot dog!

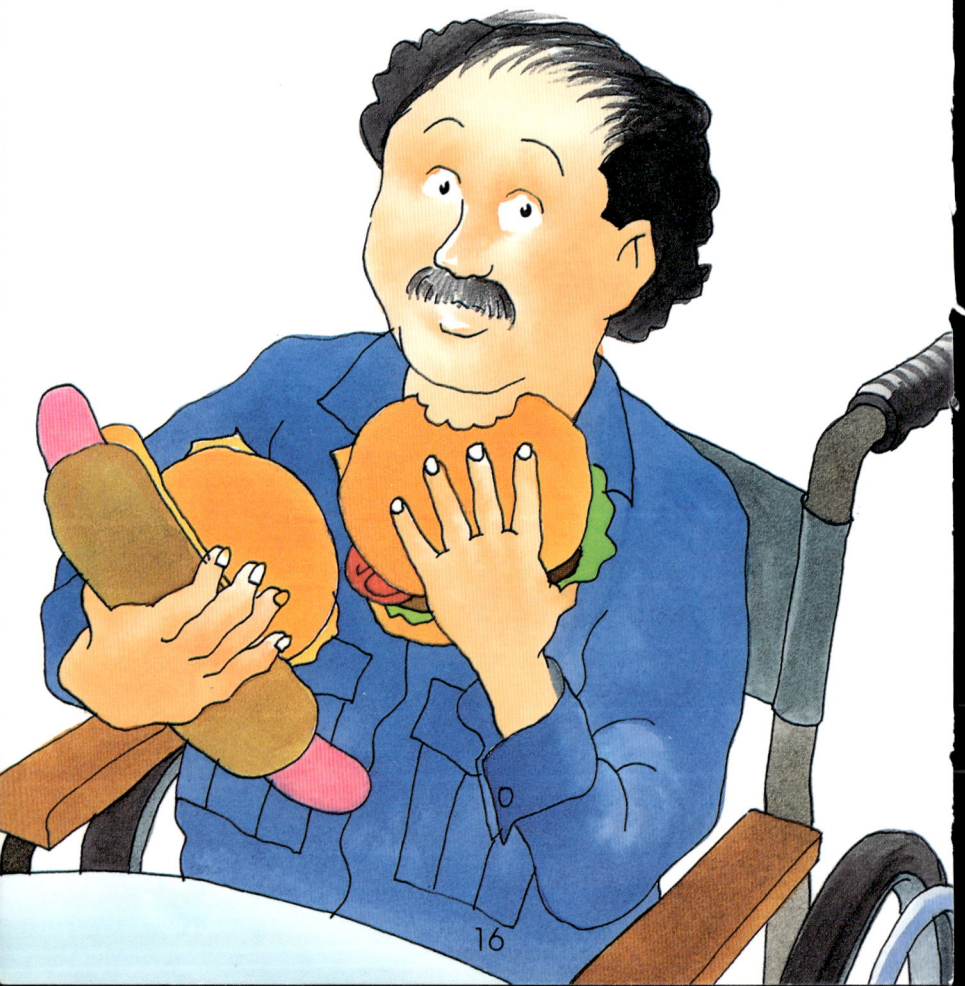